5 basic facts
about money
I learned before
I was 18

Zhou Wang, MBA

Vanguard's Top Ten: 10 mutual funds for the rest of your life

IAN Books

An IAN Books paperback

Published by
IAN Books
41 Watchung Plaza, B242
Montclair, NJ 07042

Copyright © 2016 IAN Books

Cover photo: SY Joseph Conrad by Piotr Berliński

Special sales for educational use by nonprofits.
IANBooksEditor@yahoo.com

ISBN-13: 978-1534665545

ISBN-10: 1534665544

Library of Congress Control Number: 2016944543

Dewey 332.024

1. Investments. 2. Finance, Personal.
I. Wang, Zhou 1948-. II. Title.

IAN Books at Amazon.com

Wealth Without Wall Street:
Buy Direct -- Avoid the Commissions, Fees, Loads

The Insiders' Guides to Buying Discount Financial Services:
Buy Direct and Save $3,000 Every Year

Drop Your Insurance:
Buy Only What You Need

Create Financial Freedom Using Your Wealth Reserve™:
Fix your financial life

The Simple Financial Life:
How to get what you want without going into debt and living paycheck to paycheck

Build Wealth Without Extra Money or Time:
You don't need to budget or get an extra job

Leah's Money Book:
"I want to control my own money."

The Marriage Money Book:
Start Right Together Right

Build Your Own $2,000,000 Tax-FREE Wealth Reserve™:
Self-insure Self-fund your lifestyle

Stop wasting $3,000 every year:
101
financial products **_NOT_** to buy and why

Wealth:
What every high school graduate needs to know in the 21st century

Contents

Interactions create wealth

I was lucky. This is the story of how I learned the **basic facts about money** from my Uncle Wei by age 18. Since I began at age 12 and I am not a genius, I think every child can get the basics in high school. I believe that the basics of money are as important as the basics of history, math, English, and the rest of high school.

I learned about money early. I don't mean learning how to open a bank account or balance a checkbook. I mean how to use money to create a financial base so we can afford a car, house, business, and retirement without borrowing. I haven't had to worry about having money during my adult life. I was not born rich but learned to invest early. My uncle gave me lessons at each birthday. I listened to him because he had a nice car and nice clothes. He lived in the better part of town. And yet he was not that much older or smarter than I was. Yet, later, I found out he was a multimillionaire.

At my birthday for 12 years, Uncle Wei ("Way") gave me $25. He showed me 12 of the top stocks on the Dow. He explained how a company made money: they sell things people need for more than the cost and pay me part of the profits. He explained that I could put the $25 in the bank or I could become an owner of these companies. I could learn about how they interacted with customers to make money by watching them closely.

He tried to emphasize that it was the interaction (sales) that created profits—and I get part of them—a dividend. Leaving my money in the bank would not help me learn about money and how it can work for me. He stressed the *interaction* part because he said interactions are how the world creates new things.

Uncle Wei told me about General Electric, Coca-Cola, and IBM etc over the next few years. He asked me to read articles he sent me during the years. His brokerage account held the stocks I picked. He would later transfer them to me when I could open my own account at age 18.

I asked about the 12 he picked. Apparently, there are too many things that can go wrong with the prospects for just one company so he said we have a better chance of success if we invest in 12.

Later I would learn that the chance of picking one winning stock out of all of them is 1 in 3,000. By age 15 I was learning about changes in interactions of these companies. They sold different things to some of the same folks and had to control sales with price, promotion, and placement. I had received dividends which I thought was really neat. I remember asking whether the dividends would continue. I wanted to know if I could predict how much I would receive by age 21. If these companies I owned continued to make money, how much would I have next year, in 5 years, 10 years, 20 years?

My uncle told me that if I reinvested the dividends to buy more shares, he would show me how to estimate how much I would have in the future. If my stock was worth $40 then and the dividend was $0.24 and we assumed Coke kept growing, he said we would use probabilities to see the range of values in the future. It turned out that the drink maker blew out all the promising technology firms.

I noticed that Warren Buffett made the same point recently, again with Coke stock. He said a person or family who bought Coke stock in 1919 when Coke stock first went on sale would have over $10 million in their account now. As the company grew, it would pay dividends and sometimes give me two stocks for each one that I owned before.

In the past, my stocks have split 3 for 1, 2 for 1 and paid dividends from 1 to 33 cents every 3 months. At each birthday, I got more money for stocks but I usually let the dividends buy more of the same company. In the past, my uncle actually got a stock certificate which I framed for my wall. They don't do that anymore.

So back when I was 14 or so I was estimating how much my stock would be worth in the future. I was introduced to the time value of money and probabilities. If my companies paid dividends of a certain amount and once and a while the stock split 2 for 1, I could look up on a table what they might be worth.

I would only know the most likely amount, not the exact. I would have between this amount and that amount. The sixties were a tumultuous time for companies so I learned they can rise by 24% and fall by 10%. Overall the value of my stocks rose about 7% a year. So if I started with $25 they would be worth between $27 and $29 about HALF the time. If I kept investing, they could grow to $180 to $190 in 5 years, $380 to $440 in 10 and $1000 to $1400 in 20 years. HALF the time they were worth the middle amount.

Probabilities and the time value of money were things my uncle taught me even though I didn't know the real names of them when I was younger. The time value of money is the name for how money grows when it is put to work and earns interest. It also can account for inflation—a 1ˢᵗ class stamp costs more today than years ago. We can estimate how much in the future.

Doing these calculations was difficult then even though I loved math. Today we have calculators and programs to do the work for us. http://www.moneychimp.com/calculator/compound_interest_calculator.htm But it is a strange fact that most of us never use these tools because we never were exposed to them in school. Probability is a topic covered even less than compounding in school. Yet saving and investing are more fundamental than the simple algebra and geometry courses our school children labor over today.

If every school child learned the value of investing and its opposite—the value LOST by credit card interest payments—the world would be a better place financially for everyone but bankers. We would all use compounding to grow our cash, first. We would never use credit card loans for anything we buy.

My friend Dan gives this example: many people will have to pay $161 per month for 10+ years to pay off the average debt of $10,050 at 15%. They will spend at least $19,360 to pay off that $10,050. (If their rate is 25%, they will pay $25,080 for $10,050.) They pay almost *double* for that same $10,050! bankrate.com

But that's not all—THE **REAL COST** IS MORE!

Think of it. If they did not have to use that $161 each month to pay off the $10,050 and $9,310 in interest, they would be able to use the $161 per month to make money. They could have made about *$37,407* in the 10 years using a mutual fund. So the REAL cost of that $10,050 debt is actually $56,496!! The lender gets the $19,360 (to pay the debt over time) and **they gave up** earning $37,407 from the $161 payment per month for 10 years. They gave up the down payment on a house! Confirm by using the calculator: http://www.moneychimp.com/calculator/compound_interest_calculator.htm

That $10,050 in debt costs most people over $56,000!
FIVE TIMES MORE

Making $250 per month **work** for 10 years in our investment account, our 'bank', can provide about $50,000, enough for a home down payment, car, vacation, etc. You will have contributed $30,000 ($3,000 for 10 years) for that $50,000. You can borrow from your 'bank' to pay cash for anything. It is special cash. **Your** 'bank' cash is worth 40% more than you paid for it.

I was lucky to have someone who could explain investing to me at an age when we usually start saving. As a young person I learned about the **power of compounding**. Almost everyone saves because they are not able to buy what they want NOW (unless they are the spoiled rich). I wanted to buy a better bike than my parents could afford. I had to work and save for it.

The difference for me was that after saving and buying the bike of my dreams, I understood a way to do this for everything. I did it for a car, later a house, a rental house, and more stocks in my choice of companies and finally serious money in mutual funds. When I got my first well-paying job, I maxed out my 401k with FREE money matched by my employer. I also opened an IRA and Roth IRA as soon as they were offered in the 70s and 90s.

I was lucky because I had an uncle that knew about money and cared enough to help me. Most parents care but don't know about investing successfully. They follow Wall Street's myths. There are just not enough money smart uncles to go around I guess.

I give this chart to everyone I work with because it shows what is possible, not guaranteed. The probability of them reaching their goals by investing (not trading) on a regular basis over time is almost 100%. The probability of reaching their goals by saving in a bank is almost 0%. I "guarantee" it.

Compounding is a basic fact about money I hope you use!

Monthly Accumulation at 12% per year										
	5	10	15	20	25	30	35	40	45	50
$100	$8,167	$23,004	$49,958	$98,925	$187,884	$349,496	$643,095	$1,176,477	$2,145,469	$3,905,834
$200	$16,334	$46,008	$99,916	$197,850	$375,768	$698,992	$1,286,190	$2,352,954	$4,290,938	$7,811,668
$300	$24,501	$69,012	$149,874	$296,775	$563,652	$1,048,488	$1,929,285	$3,529,431	$6,436,408	$11,717,502
$500	$40,835	$115,020	$249,790	$494,625	$939,420	$1,747,480	$3,215,475	$5,882,385	$10,727,346	$19,529,169

1

Tax-FREE is better than taxable

When Uncle Wei transferred all my stocks to my own brokerage account in 1968, I was mortified to find out I had to start paying taxes on the earnings even though I was reinvesting the dividends. After all, I was not using the dividends. Why did I need to pay tax on them? It was the same in my savings account.

The problem with saving and investing was that we had to pay taxes on the earnings (until recently). Even with our 401k and IRAs, we will have to pay taxes eventually. We don't get to keep all our money even though we had to sacrifice to make it grow. I got used to paying since I had a good job. Later, when 401ks were offered, I was happy to defer the taxes on my income but I still had to pay on my brokerage dividends and interest.

The solution to our investing problem came in 1997. Senators Packwood and Roth created the Roth IRA. This tax-FREE account provides the protection we need to allow our contributions to compound without taxation every year *AND* later when we take them out, we never have to pay taxes on the earnings, dividends and interest we earn on our money. We don't even pay the tax-advantaged capital gains rate of the wealthy!

Ben Franklin was wrong! Only death is certain, not taxes. The only thing we give up with this account is an immediate tax deduction. However, compare the value of paying a little more tax (15% on $3,000) now with paying ZERO on $30,000 gains later. We can spend $30,000 tax-FREE for every $3,000 a year we contribute over time. We can see the fantastic advantage we now have. Pay tax on $3,000 a year now and pay $0 on 1,000,000 later. This is a better deal than most wealthy people have.

Tax-FREE accumulation and tax-FREE income after age 59 1/2 is a huge bonus. It is like receiving $300,000 FREE on our $1 million account. Also, because we already paid tax on the contributions, we pay no tax if we take contributions out for emergencies. This can make a big impact on our borrowing costs when we take money out to buy an appliance, a car repair, a down payment or temporary living expenses.

This special account is the IRS §408A trust. We have to follow the rules to gain this amazing tax advantage but the Roth IRA rules are pretty simple—taxed money goes in and tax-FREE earnings come out after age 59 ½. We can take our contributions out anytime. https://www.law.cornell.edu/uscode/text/26/408A

Tax-FREE v Taxable

Why is this account special? Every other type of investment account requires that taxes be paid now or later. Mutual funds declare gains each year just like a bank CD and we need to pay tax. Our retirement accounts and annuities are tax-deferred. We pay tax when we take money out. Even life insurance with cash value requires taxes to be paid unless it is a death benefit to heirs. Even assets like individual stocks or ETFs or our own company equity held for long term gains will require taxes eventually when sold. The gains in this account are FREE—no tax ever.

Contributions are limited to $5,500 (2016), but may rise in future years. http://www.irs.gov/publications/p590a There are income limits of $132,000 (2016) or $194,000 married. We make our deposit to our Roth IRA **account** automatic so we can't forget to do it each month. We buy more shares when the price is low.

We may also invest in our employer's Roth 401k if it is offered. The contributions grow tax FREE forever. We can contribute more to this account. We will have tax-FREE income from the account later. Contributions to a regular 401k can be converted later. We can limit taxes by converting small portions of our 401k or regular IRA each year.

There are no limits on an employee's income in determining if he or she can make designated Roth 401(k) contributions. If we decide to invest $6,000 a year for about 26 years in a low-cost stock fund inside our employer's Roth 401k plan, we could accumulate $1 million with NO income taxation to pay on the earnings. The tax savings might be worth an extra 30% since our federal and state tax payments are avoided. We **Keep More of What We Earn**.

The catch: If we take the *earnings* out before age 59.5, we must pay income tax, unless we use $10,000 for our first home, are disabled, or die. The account must be open at least 5 years to take money out. However, if we take out *contributions*, we pay no tax. If we pay our 'loan' back to our own account, we can still reach our goal. The hard part is leaving our money alone to grow tax-FREE.

The rules for the use of our Roth IRA account are manageable by ourselves. We don't need an advisor. They are found at irs.gov/retirement/article/0,,id=137307,00.html. Our account trustee can answer most questions. We don't need to pay an attorney. All of the large low-cost mutual funds firms are trustees. We will discuss the best firms available below.

It is important to pick a trustee with the least costs since over time the annual costs can really destroy our accumulations. For instance, if we use a brokerage firm as trustee, we might have to pay 2% or more each year on the balance. The difference is huge: up to 63% of our potential total is taken in fees.

If both spouses have a low-cost account with contributions of $250 a month for about 26 years, they could accumulate $1,000,000. If they use a high-cost broker/advisor, both accounts may hit only $500,000. Depending on earnings of 8-10% using a broker/advisor (fees of 2-3% per year), they could really hurt themselves. We need to watch the costs.

We can open our account at any age as long as we have *earned* income—stock dividends or interest do not count. Any job will do. We don't even need a job requiring a W-2 to prove it. A part-time, weekend or night job will do. Any cash-only work will also qualify. Accountants recommend that receipts and records be maintained. We could even work for ourselves in a home-office business. This also provides a tax advantage in retirement.

Nontaxable distributions from a Roth IRA won't affect our eligibility for a child's student aid. Later, in retirement, this money won't raise the taxes on our Social Security benefits.

We can make contributions to both our individual Roth IRA and our Roth account at work (401k). The limits change each year, so check Pub 590: https://www.irs.gov/publications/p590a/index.html The rules are pretty simple: pay smaller tax on contributions now in exchange for NO tax on huge gains later—over time, $99,000 is taxed so $901,000 is tax-FREE. As the account grows, we can use the contributions to avoid paying interest to banks for our major purchases. We earn interest, we don't pay interest.

Range of annual returns of stocks, 1950 – 2000

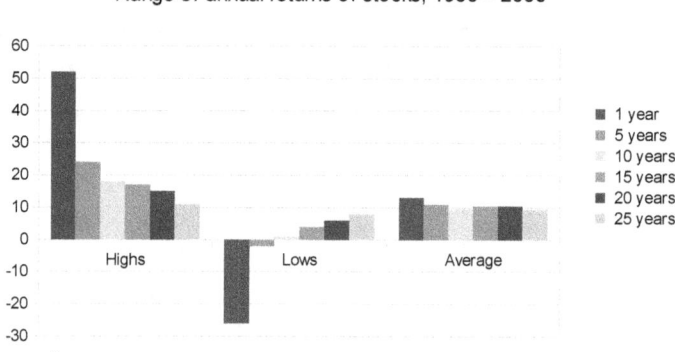

This account is the perfect tax shelter for working people. And it is simple to set up and run each year. In the future, we can spend $30,000 tax-FREE for every $3,000 we invest each year.

Building a $1 million tax-FREE account takes time. If we own a business, it would take a lifetime. We would have to find and sell the right product to the right customer in a profitable manner. It is difficult to come up with a completely new product or way to sell it like Apple has done.

By investing in growing companies, we are silent owners receiving dividends, stock splits and appreciation. Over time, there is no better investment. There are few investments that we can easily buy that have the same long-term annual returns of stocks of growing companies. The chart above shows that for all periods over 10 years, the returns have been positive over 10%. It also assumes that there are no taxes or fees in the account.

The graph below makes it pretty clear that in order to accumulate $1,000,000 from monthly contributions, we must buy and hold the securities of growing companies worldwide, at cost, AND pay **zero** tax on the growth to maximize compounding. We can see clearly that investing in growing company stocks is more likely to get us to our goal in our lifetime than investing in government bonds or a bank savings account.

This graph shows the accumulation over time without paying taxes each year on our earnings or annual fees to an advisor or broker. It does show that over most periods greater than 10 years, our account value grows more with stocks.

If an investment requires taxes to be paid each year, this cancels some of the compounding effect on the total accumulation over time. Since we wish to reach $1 million as soon as possible, we must use a tax-advantaged account to hold our low-cost investments. Depending on our tax bracket (taxable income) we may reduce our total accumulation by over half because we lose the compounding effect. We give up HALF to taxes over time. Most retirement accounts are tax-DEFERRED; not tax-FREE. Taxes have to be paid sometime.

As you have probably guessed, the wealthy have already figured out how to pay less tax on their wealth. The American tax system taxes earned income at higher rates than investment income. Plus we must pay federal and state income taxes, excise taxes, Social Security and Medicare taxes, perhaps unemployment and disability income taxes as well as sales tax on most goods.

For the wealthy, like Warren Buffett, with $65 billions of assets, most of his income is from his company stock gains and dividends. He admitted, "I pay at a lower overall tax rate than all of my office employees." He pays only 17% **total** tax. They pay 33%. Listen and weep: http://www.youtube.com/watch?v=Cu5B-2LoC4s.

Most of us have income which is taxed as earned income and goes straight to the government before we have a chance to pay less tax. Even self-employed people must pay taxes as they go—at least once a quarter. Only the wealthy and large companies can afford most tax avoidance schemes. Fortunately, Congress created one for working people. The Roth IRA lets us avoid income tax on the earnings altogether. And we don't need to go offshore.

Basic fact
Tax-FREE is better than taxable account for building wealth.

Various investment accumulations

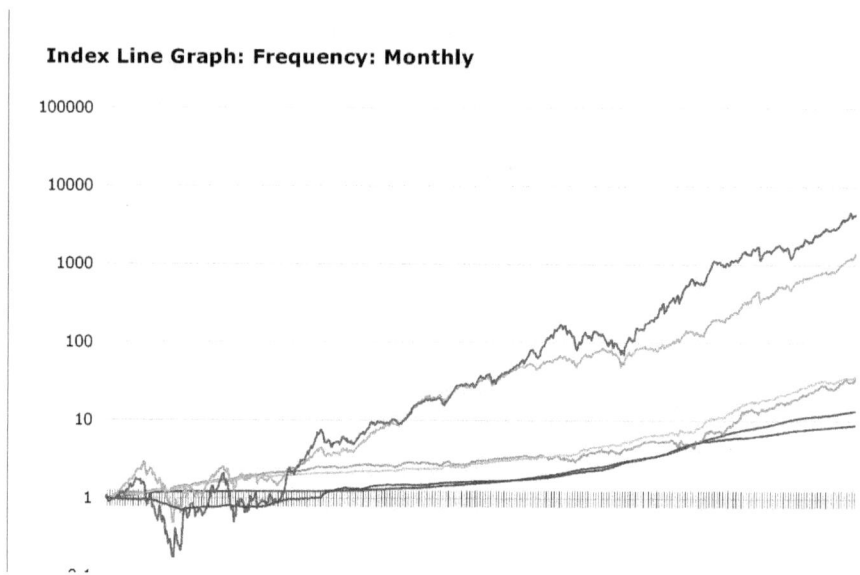

Index Line Graph: Frequency: Monthly

Top line—Small Cap Stocks
2nd line—Large Cap Stocks (S&P 500)
3rd line—US Long-term Corporate Bonds
4th line—Intermediate-term Government Bonds
5th line—US 30 day Government T-bills
6th line—US inflation

Courtesy: Dr. Campbell R. Harvey http://www.duke.edu/~charvey/

2

Lifetime of patience

Uncle Wei started my education in money by explaining how business works. I was fascinated by stereo systems at the time. I built my own amp (from a kit) and speaker enclosure I designed myself—an "infinite baffle" type. Wei asked me to explain how my pretend company would build and sell my design for a profit. I learned first hand from his example, how to grow a business. I learned patience as he explained how we make sales in a territory, expand to other areas and grow the business.

It takes a lot of hard work and a lot of patience to grow a business. It was a lot of fun too. We used a kind of business plan he modified from his own business. There were times when he said things grew slowly or not at all—but you still have expenses—and times when you couldn't keep up with demand.

If investing is like this, it will take a lot of patience to become successful. He had explained that investing is becoming a silent owner of a business. So when I bought Coke stock in the 60s, my uncle compared it to my "speaker company." Opening markets cost money and that is where my $25 would probably go. If Coke were successful, I would get part of the profits as dividends for the rest of my life if I kept the stock. He went over how reinvesting the dividends buys more stock so I get more dividends.

Compounding is the secret to wealth, he said. We must find a way to encourage compounding. Compounding is money making money on itself. Dividends reinvested in the same company are the logical conclusion. Adding more money periodically also encourages compounding. Finally, it takes time for a company to grow. It takes time for our money to work and produce dividends.

We must be patient. Fidelity recently examined its most successful client accounts. Guess what it found? The most successful investors had either forgotten about their account or died. We must not touch our money. It's working. Let it work!

Patience is important in life and in building wealth. I have seen in my career that most investors are not patient so most investors will not have enough later. In fact, the average investor earns only 3.79% annually (vs market returns of 11.06%) according to DALBAR's Quantitative Analysis of Investor Behavior.

Mr Buffett's strategy of patience earns 19.7% compounded over time. **He does not buy and sell**—he owns the stocks of companies for a long time. He is NOT a Wall Street trader. Most investors jump from one *already* popular stock or mutual fund to another. Each time they do this, they are basically paying at the higher price AFTER the security has proved successful. Each time they are disappointed and then sell at a lower price. Every buy and sell transaction costs them a commission or fee, reducing their gains even more. They earn 3.79% while Buffett earns 19.7%.

We must be silent owners. Once we start investing in securities or mutual funds, **we do nothing** to stop the growth of our account. We patiently let the market provide our wealth. Buffett has been patient for over 40 years and has grown his initial investment of $6,000 (from paper routes) to $65 **billion**. You don't need to do a thing to *grow* your money in the stock market.

You and I will never become wealthy trying to find the right stocks to earn what Buffett has earned. He studied value investing at Columbia University. Most importantly, he knew at what price to buy Coke, GEICO, Fruit of the Loom, Benjamin Moore, Acme Bricks, Burlington Northern, etc. berkshirehathaway.com/

So what can average people do? Buffett gave us the answer.

"A very low-cost index is going to beat a majority of the amateur-managed money or professionally-managed money."

He says buy a low-cost index fund. That's it! **Simplicity** itself. We earn 10-12% by doing what Buffett has recommended for the average investor: Buy and hold simple low-cost funds owning a bunch of stocks. Investing becomes effortless. We follow his advice and buy and hold **low-cost** high-return stock mutual funds and wait. We have to be patient and **do NOTHING**.

Today, we can thank John Bogle, Vanguard founder, who created low-cost index funds in 1975. The economist, Paul Samuelson, said, "My prayer has been answered." Buffett says if we **hold** a low-cost index fund, we will beat Wall Street's professional money managers. This is against everything we have been told by all the "smart" people in media. It is counter-intuitive to **just leave our money alone**. But smart investors take his advice because it works, ignoring the hype.

My Own Brokerage Account

Market Returns	Account Value		Year	
	$5,000 *			
37%	$12,604	0	1975	
24%	$20,837	1	1976	
-8%	$23,034	2	1977	
6%	$28,868	3	1978	
18%	$38,020	4	1979	
				Paid $1,000 for car
32%	$55,731	5	1980	
-5%	$56,934	6	1981	
22%	$74,584	7	1982	
21%	$95,328	8	1983	
6%	$105,500	9	1984	
32%	$129,804	10	1985	
				Paid $15000 for house down payment
19%	$159,465	11	1986	
5%	$171,848	12	1987	
17%	$205,976	13	1988	
32%	$277,433	14	1989	
-3%	$273,184	15	1990	
31%	$363,373	16	1991	
8%	$396,979	17	1992	
10%	$441,296	18	1993	
2%	$454,406	19	1994	
38%	$632,877	20	1995	
				Laid off
23%	$772,138	21	1996	
				$3,000 vacation
33%	$970,594	22	1997	
				$56,350 kid's college
28%	$1,232,360	23	1998	
				Paid $10,000 for home repairs
21%	$1,491,156	24	1999	
-9%	$1,356,952	25	2000	
-12%	$1,195,475	26	2001	
-22%	$931,275	27	2002	
29%	$1,201,344	28	2003	
11%	$1,333,492	29	2004	
5%	$1,400,167	30	2005	
16%	$1,624,194	31	2006	

*Inflation adjusted dollars.

When my uncle and I started investing it was hard to wait to see what would happen. He bought my first stocks in his account.

Later I opened an account and moved my stocks.

Luckily by then I was consumed with work and a girlfriend. I did not think about what happened in the account except when I got my dividends—4 times a year. I did nothing because there was nothing to do. Uncle Wei said, "Just wait."

I invested with my employer's pension plan. First a profit-sharing plan ESOP. Later they had a 401k plan but the options carried high fees. My uncle had warned me about high fee securities. They had no low-cost index options.

We can earn 10-12% over time by using a stock market index in a low-cost mutual fund. Why? Vanguard is *NOT* owned by Wall Street. It is owned by us--its shareholders. All services are provided *at cost* for our benefit. Bogle's vision was one of a fiduciary--a steward of our "mutual" assets. He learned that most professionals can't win long term because they must **always** take their profits from **our** earnings. Wall Street increases profits by adding assets. No one knows which businesses will grow quickly unless they have insider information. So we earn less because we pay more.

Bogle saw that an index fund can beat managers by just making par—the average. By earning the average returns of 10-12% a year we will become wealthy. Each of our $3,000 annual investments would be worth about $30,000 over 20 years in a diversified group of businesses like those in Vanguard funds.

Most wealthy people are not speculators. They don't bet the ranch on a hot tip. That is gambling. AND it doesn't make you rich. They don't waste their money on high-fee products that brokers or advisors sell. Patience is all we need to let our 'seed money' grow over time. All we have to do is set up auto investing and forget it.

Wise investors know they will never be able to pick the right companies for the future. Wall Street tempts us by claiming they know. Some of us follow their advice and pay dearly. The industry tells us that we need them to get rich but we give up $560 billions of our earnings every year. We help them more than ourselves. Trading does NOT benefit us. pbs.org/moyers/journal/09282007/

Compounding—the real source of Buffett's success—works only if we leave our money alone. **Simple but profound**. Easy, but hard to do. It is like playing the lottery every week but instead of losing every week our "bet" compounds into $1 million eventually.

As Buffett said,

"My wealth has come from a combination of living in America, some lucky genes, and **compound interest**."

When I work with clients I try to make it clear that we must let *money go to work for us*. We are the owners. We must learn to be patient and let it work for us. We simply buy and hold low-cost mutual stock funds.

Investing, not speculating is all about putting our money in actual businesses that are growing so that in the future we can get our money back multiplied many times over. We invest in a number of successful businesses so if one fails, we still earn 10-12% a year. We want to pay few fees or taxes so that our account compounds at the full 10-12%. We want to invest a fixed amount like $250 a month (about $9 a day) automatically so we can **set it and forget it**. Do nothing.

Today, when we buy and hold our low-cost mutual fund investments in a special account, the earnings are tax-FREE. That means we can accumulate $1 million from our $250 a month in about 33 years. We could only do that by using a NO tax, LOW fee account. The earnings are reinvested and compounded over time.

I have been in financial services for over 20 years. Wealthy people usually have their own business and reinvest their profits back in the business. Most don't know a thing about investing but know that they can't beat the market by buying and selling a growing business every month or quarter like Wall Street claims.

The key factor in building wealth is letting our money make money. Mr Buffett cites the **miracle of compounding**. We can do the same in a tax-FREE account, paying low fees. Taxes and fees take away the miracle of compounding.

We don't pay taxes on the amount our account earns every year. We don't pay high fees on the balance of our account every year. We invest in a proven long-term investment—shares of growing companies worldwide.

If our investing is done automatically, we have a better chance of success. Automatic investing is simplicity itself. We can't miss making a contribution. The people who succeed at building wealth are those who NEVER stop saving and investing.

Both of you invest in high-earning securities over time. We let the miracle of compounding work. We pay $99,000 in 33 years for $1,000,000. We don't stop investing when the market goes up or down. We make investing automatic. The miracle happens because we do NOTHING. We have more because we pay less!

Building wealth requires **patience**. If you are self-employed, you understand that it takes time to build a business. You have to have the right product and then find the customers to serve at a price that enables you to earn a living and a profit to expand.

If you work for others, you don't have to be a genius to become financially independent. Wealthy people control their spending by various methods. Some have goals and budgets that help them keep their spending and investing habits. Some are thrifty and don't spend more than they make. Most use CPAs not brokers.

Wealthy people have learned that there is **no quick way** to become wealthy. The ones you hear about on TV are the exceptionally lucky. Most, like my plumber, worked and saved for years. Accumulating assets requires the investing habit. Most wealthy people learned the habit and saw that the habit paid off over time. Their money compounds and is taxed at reduced rates.

Building wealth is more about **NOT** doing something with your investments. Activity in investing usually is the result of fear or greed. Buffett said he holds stocks "forever." $40 to $50 million, he says. https://www.youtube.com/watch?v=XG945hoLLhk

People with assets cultivate **patience**. They don't panic when their account goes down. In fact, they buy more assets when on sale and others are selling. They know they cannot build a small fortune overnight with a quick buy and sell strategy. **Patience** allows assets to "grow by themselves." Note above that my account keeps growing even after falling some years. I never lost money because I did NOT sell in the down years!

People with assets understand that to build wealth they need to keep their money working. They do this by buying only the products they need today and improve their future by buying assets that "grow by themselves." The chart of client Tom below illustrates the growth of $3,000 a year from 1962 to 2003.

Basic fact

Compounding is the source of wealth and it requires our patience. It is hard to do nothing with our money. But we must let it work.

Actual client, Tom's account, investing $3,000 per year, 1962-2003

24%	3,720
16%	7,795
12%	12,091
-10%	13,582
24%	20,561
11%	26,153
-8%	26,821
4%	31,013
14%	38,775
19%	49,713
-14%	45,333
-26%	35,766
37%	53,110
24%	69,576
-8%	66,770
6%	73,956
18%	90,809
32%	123,827
-5%	120,486
22%	150,653
21%	185,920
6%	200,255
32%	268,297
19%	322,843
5%	342,135
17%	403,808
32%	536,987
-3%	523,787
31%	690,091
8%	748,538
10%	826,692
2%	846,286
38%	1,172,015
23%	1,445,268
33%	1,926,197
28%	2,469,372
21%	2,991,570
-9%	2,725,059
-12%	2,403,420
-22%	1,874,601
29%	2,412,905

3

Compound high earnings over time

2015 Total Return	Fund	Long-term Return	Longevity
1.4%	500 Index	10.8%*	since 1976
-21.5%	Energy	10.3%	since 1984
-3.3%	Extended Market Idx	10.6%	since 1987
12.7%	Health	17.3%	since 1984
-0.7%	International Growth	10.3%	since 1981
2.6%	PRIMECAP	13.5%	since 1984
-3.6%	Small Cap Index	10.5%	since 1960
1.3%	Wellesley Income	9.9%	since 1970
-3.3%	Windsor	11.3%	since 1958
-3.2%	Windsor II	10.6%	since 1985
-1.7%	Average	11.5%	

*Average Annual Returns as of 12/31/15.

Uncle Wei taught me about money by showing me how a business works and makes a profit. This is what many people who "play" the market fail to grasp. Yes, there are lucky people who have made quick money just like there are gamblers who win. But most don't because trading and gambling are "loser's games."

The wealthy people I know earn 10% to 12% on their money on a consistent basis. They are not gamblers. They own all ten Vanguard funds and receive 11.5% total return with less risk than owning just one fund. When one fund is down, others are up.

Compounding high earnings is key. The rich get richer—the top 1% take 23.5% of all income (up from 8.9%). And, as many millionaires have said, "the first million is the hardest." If both of you start with $3,000, it will take you about 20 years of investing $6,000 a year in stock funds to reach $500,000 (and only in a tax-FREE low-fee account).

However, when you reach a **1/2** million dollars, you only have to double your money to reach $1 million. Investors in stock mutual funds, earning 10-12% on average, do this in about 8 years without adding new money. Your low-fee tax-FREE accounts make it easier to reach your goals. You pay no advisor costs because you use a simple strategy and let the markets do what they do.

Compounding of high earnings means that we make money on our last period's accumulations. The progression looks like Tom's account values above. Notice that our balance can double in a few good years. This happens because we are not just adding money each month, but adding up to 38% of the previous year's accumulation to our balance. We are making money on top of our money with no extra effort on our part. During this 40 year period, this client 'lost' money some years. In fact, he lost 14% and then 26% back to back, but then made 37% and 24%.

Wealthy people do not panic and sell. They have learned that compounding over the long term is the only way they can build wealth. To reach their goal, they know there will be setbacks. No business grows steadily upward all the time. They have seen the losses before and they don't sell their assets in a panic. They remain **patient**.

We will buy assets that "grow by themselves." We will have security because our ***purchasing power*** will grow over time. If we doubt that the wealthy invest in the stock market for security, take a look at the long-term returns for various Vanguard mutual funds where they put their money. These funds have provided investors with $1,000,000 or more for their retirement. During the recent recession, Vanguard had inflows not outflows.

2014 Total Return	Fund	Long-term Return	Longevity
13.5%	500 Index	11.1%*	since 1976
-14.3%	Energy	11.5%	since 1984
7.4%	Extended Market Idx	11.1%	since 1987
28.5%	Health	17.4%	since 1984
-5.6%	International Growth	10.6%	since 1981
18.7%	PRIMECAP	13.9%	since 1984
7.5%	Small Cap Index	9.3%	since 1960
8.1%	Wellesley Income	10.1%	since 1970
11.8%	Windsor	11.6%	since 1958
11.2%	Windsor II	11.1%	since 1985
8.7%	Average	11.8%	

*Average Annual Returns as of 12/31/14.

This kind of security comes from our simple strategy—automatic contributions … and patience. The miracle of compounding works its magic on our money when we give it TIME. The wealthy give their money time to compound.

It took this client 21 years to get to $150,000. Then it only took 14 years to get to a $1,172,015. After only 4 years, it became $3,000,000. Shortly thereafter he "lost" over a million dollars! This client stuck with it and was successful in reaching the goal but there are many who did not. Most people who are not wealthy already, have a hard time believing it can happen with their *patience*. They just don't have the experience of running a company.

If you already have a Roth IRA with significant values, you can use it to do your gift and estate planning. You don't have to take the money out beginning at age 70½, unlike the regular IRA or pension. You can let it grow. You can name your family members as beneficiaries which will extend the miracle of compounding. Obviously, as beneficiary, your grandchild could just liquidate the account and thus lose the value of their "Gift of a Lifetime." Wealthy people use a knowledgable attorney to make sure their wealth passes to those who will make the most of it.

Basic fact

Compounding high earnings creates wealth. Compounding requires patience. Patience is the hard part.

The annual returns of growing companies

Range of annual returns of stocks, 1950 – 2000

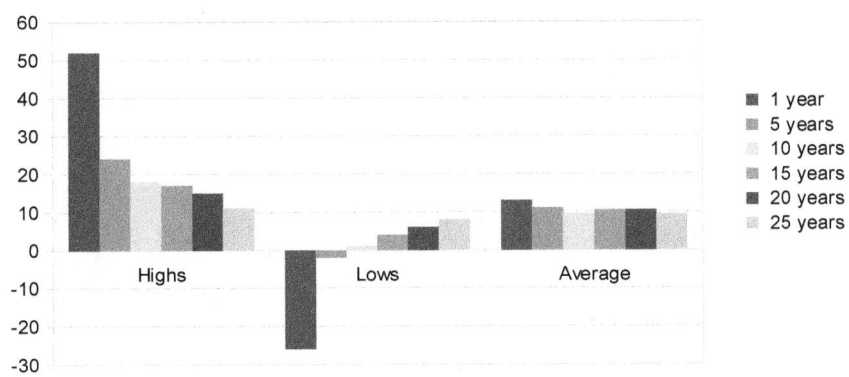

4

Automatic investing

The Value of Starting Early

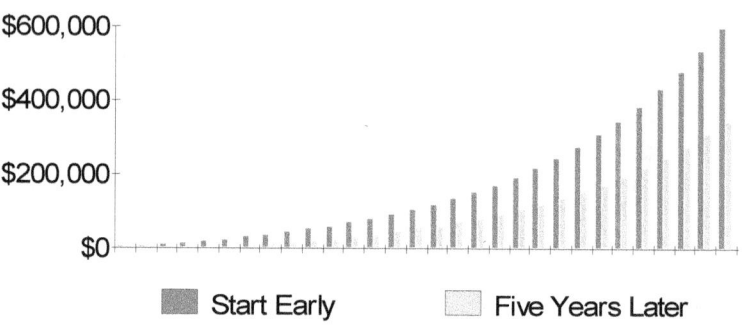

Uncle Wei showed me how investing can fail. When he began putting money in the stock market, he did it with his occasional bonus money. His account records showed that he bought $10,000 worth of Coke the month AFTER it had split 3 for 1. If he had been buying stock on a regular basis, he would have three times the number of shares.

We avoid bad timing and overpaying for stocks by buying every month. We avoid procrastination too. We don't wait for the market to drop to invest. Auto investing can stop us from overpaying. If we invest $250 a month, we buy fewer shares when the price is high and more shares when it is low. This goes for dividends too. When we set up our account, we can have the firm reinvest dividends automatically—and usually at no cost.

At first I didn't think this was important. My 24 cent dividend back in the 60s was not going to buy many shares. However, today my thousands of shares produce thousands of dividends which produce thousands more shares. And I get $0 commission.

Making it automatic helps take our money emotions out of the process. If we put our investing on automatic, we don't have to *agonize every month* about sending in a check. We don't notice if our trustee debits our checking every month like a bill or our employer plan reduces our taxable income every payday.

People tend to panic when the market falls if they get used to monitoring their account every month in order to send in a check. They think "the market rose on Friday, so I should wait to send my check." By the time you execute the buy, the market may be higher. There were **only 20 trading days** that made up the 10% annual market returns from 1994-2013. If you or your broker missed those days, you would have earned less than a bank CD.
https://www.ifa.com/12steps/step4/missing_the_best_and_worst_days/

No "professional" or computer has been able to predict the returns for the market or for an individual firm despite research. I learned to not deceive myself into believing Wall Street hype that they can predict any future gains. Remember, on any given day or week or year, someone will have the highest total earnings. It is impossible to know who they are in advance though.

This basic fact is the lesson that the industry would NOT allow our schools to teach. This basic fact is the reason Warren Buffett, who has no way to profit from his advice to us, recommends we avoid "professionals" and use index funds on a regular basis. The market is NOT a roulette wheel. As Buffett has said,

"The market is a device for transferring money from the impatient to the patient."

When we buy we become owners of growing companies not gamblers. The market makes buying easier. For many large companies like Coke, we could buy stock directly. https://www-us.computershare.com/Investor/3x/Plans/PlansList.asp

We use a market index fund because it has a higher probability of 10-12% returns **over time** than one company. Research of financial returns over time shows that a group of global businesses will continue to grow and produce profits on an expected basis more often than one company. However, most people don't look at wealth-building in that way. Most people do not think of their accounts as a stake in many growing businesses.

I use the example of Social Security contributions. Investing is like the Social Security contributions we make every payday, the

contributions are made automatically. If they weren't mandatory, we wouldn't do it. After 30-40 years of work contributions, you end up with a schedule of benefits. The equivalent private account to reproduce the average SS benefits of $1,328/mo for the average benefit period of 20 years is $600,000. The maximum benefit is $2,663/mo. Some receive benefits to age 100 or more. Using our calculator, we can estimate how large our virtual SS account has to be. Vanguard retirement income calculator shows that you have at least $400,000 in your virtual account before taxes.
https://retirementplans.vanguard.com/VGApp/pe/pubeducation/calculators/RetirementNestEggCalc.jsf

So if you did not have a SS benefit coming to you (you were forced to pay for it), it would take an investment account of about $600,000 (before taxes) to replace your benefits. Your SS account may have $1.2 million if you receive the max benefit and live to age 100.

Just in case you can't live on $1,328 a month, you could invest $250 a month now in a Roth 401k. Your Plan administrator will deduct the amount you specify at Plan enrollment. In the same manner, we can have the Roth IRA trustee debit our checking account automatically every month.

As one client told me, "I never see the deduction, so I never miss it." Of course this client had already identified the $250 he had committed to his $2,000,000 future years ago. He says that he would just waste the $250 on a new car lease anyway. He had been doing that for years because he never took the trouble to set his goals for short-term and long-term timelines. He went through his spending with a knife. He used our *Guides* to find the $250 a month he was wasting on products and services he would never use or need. In our amazon.com/Insiders-Guides-Discount-Financial-Services/ you will find "tricks of the trade" that we insiders use to buy directly from quality financial manufacturers.

Many people have trouble keeping up the habit of investing every month. Some emergency always interupts this process. The delay in the periodic contributions causes the compounding effect to be reduced. The interruption is like starting the investment process late. The graph above shows us what starting early or not putting off the investments can do. Over time, *the delay compounds the lack of accumulation*. Starting 5 years later means ending up with HALF the amount we were shooting for. It is hard to believe that missing that $250 a month for 5 years or $15,000 can reduce our total from $600,000 to $300,000. It's easy to say **I will start later.**

This is why our contributions to the account should not pass through our hands. We should have the money taken directly from our bank account by the trustee. Contributions are after-tax so you can take them from your future without tax, when necessary. Nontaxable distributions from a Roth IRA won't affect your eligibility for student aid either. Later, in retirement, this money won't affect your Social Security benefits, which are subject to taxation depending on your income. Even municipal bonds are counted in the tax worksheet for SS benefits. irs.gov/pub/irs-pdf/p915.pdf

The second reason why this technique for developing wealth works is that when contributions are automatic, we do not have the temptation to try to time the market. Many people want to know the secret to timing the market so that they can invest right at the bottom of market cycles and sell at the peak of the market.

Unfortunately, it is a myth that we can do this. Again, this is our misconception of how building wealth works. Yes, there are lucky gamblers. However, they are the exception. We use compounding. We want to end up with $1,000,000 tax-FREE. We are silent partners in building businesses that produce dividends and gains over time. We are NOT placing our "bets"; our contributions on the red or black at the casino. We would have to win all the time.

Our account grows with steady contributions because in the month we buy shares in a mutual fund, we receive less shares when the price is high and more shares when the price is low. Studies have shown that this is better than investing our $3,000/$6,000 all at once. It is not possible to know when the shares we buy will be at their lowest cost in the year going forward. Again, over time, we will own more shares at the least cost because we are buying more when the price is low.

This can be illustrated by considering how hard it is to find the lowest price at any given time in the market. There were ONLY 40 days from 1950 to 2007 that produced 70% of all the S&P 500 index's total returns. That's 40 out of 14,528 or 0.0027. We can't possibly know when to buy into the businesses at the right time. We will lose money if we become traders who try to time the market. Traders lose money most of the time. See John Bogle's analysis in *Don't Count on It*, p 169.

The key to wealth is patience: let compounding work. We just don't know which companies and which time to invest are best. Luckily, we don't have to know. ***We just let*** our money compound the high earnings in a tax-FREE mutual fund.

Accumulations double in value every 8-10 years if they are concentrated in the top two lines below. Of course the stock market doesn't move up at 10-12% EACH year. However, our account will double and double and double so that in about 26 years, we could have ***$1/2 million each***. Notice how the account values in the chart for client Tom double—from $1 million to $2 million in 8 years, even with 3 years of losses. Of course, a million dollars will be worth less in the future because of inflation. But we will certainly appreciate our account values later no matter what our contributions are now. Consistency over time builds wealth.

Cumulative Wealth

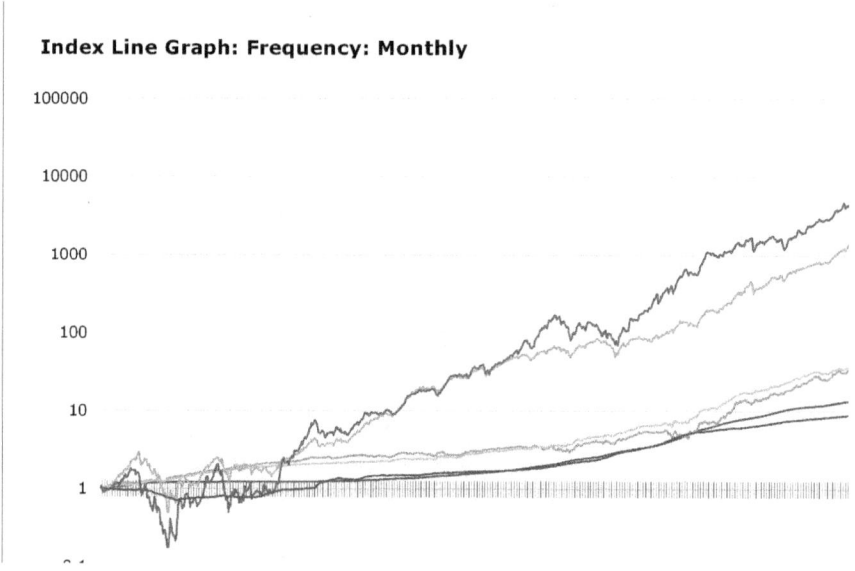

Top line—Small Cap Stocks
2nd line—Large Cap Stocks (S&P 500)
3rd line—US Long-term Corporate Bonds
4th line—Intermediate-term Government Bonds
5th line—US 30 day Government T-bills
6th line—US inflation

Courtesy: Dr. Campbell R. Harvey http://www.duke.edu/~charvey/

And the bonus of this geometric account growth is that it does not quit even after we stop adding our monthly contributions. Once the account has reached a certain mass, let's say after 20 years of $6K contributions or $120,000, it will keep compounding. Below we show you how this worked for contributions of $2,000 to a virtual account invested in the stock market over time.

We see in the chart "**Cumulative Wealth**" above that wealth accumulates at different rates depending on the type of assets we buy. For anyone who invested in smaller companies over any given 15 year period, the benefits were outstanding. For each $1,000 invested in 1940, $3,000,000 was the total return by the 1990's. Investing more cautiously in the large companies of the S&P 500, for instance, our $1,000 would have grown to almost a $1,000,00 by 2000. Yes, the lines are not perfectly straight, but growing $500 a month to $1,000,000 is definitely worth the ups and downs. Inflation is designated by the bottom line here. Putting all our money in the bank for 'safety' would accumulate at a rate represented by a line near that bottom line.

Of course, these different rates of wealth accumulation assume two important factors—NO taxes and LOW costs. We have eliminated the first killer of wealth—TAXES—by using a tax-FREE trust account. High cost "professionally" managed accounts can also kill our total accumulations. The whole financial industry is built on the extraction of these costs from our accounts. We must use low-cost stock funds to have a *Tax-FREE Retirement*.

The hard part of investing is being patient. If we put our monthly contributions and dividends on automatic, we are more likely to meet our goals. We set it and forget it.
Earl Crawley, parking attendant, did it:
http://www.youtube.com/watch?v=XD0svDGyLWU

Basic fact
On automatic, we forget we are investing in our future and thus we actually create it. Irony of ironies!

$2,000 Annual Stock Market Investment 1950- '70- '80- '90- 2013

Year	Returns	Balance	Balance	Balance	Balance
		$2,000			
1950	31%	$2,620			
1951	24%	$5,729			
1952	18%	$9,120			
1953	-1%	$11,009			
1954	52%	$19,773			
1955	31%	$28,523			
1956	5%	$32,049			
1957	-11%	$30,304			
1958	43%	$46,194			
1959	12%	$53,978			
1960	1%	$56,538			
1961	26%	$73,757			
1962	-8%	$69,697			
1963	24%	$88,904			
1964	16%	$105,449			
1965	12%	$120,342			
1966	-10%	$110,108			
1967	24%	$139,014			
1968	11%	$156,526			
1969	-8%	$145,844	2,000		
1970	4%	$153,757	2,080		
1971	14%	$177,563	4,651		
1972	19%	$213,681	7,915		
1973	-14%	$185,485	8,527		
1974	-26%	$138,739	7,790		
1975	37%	$192,813	13,412		
1976	24%	$241,568	19,111		
1977	-8%	$224,082	19,422		
1978	6%	$239,647	22,707		
1979	18%	$285,144	29,155	2,000	
1980	32%	$379,030	41,124	2,640	
1981	-5%	$361,978	40,968	4,408	
1982	22%	$444,053	52,421	7,818	
1983	21%	$539,724	65,850	11,879	
1984	6%	$574,228	71,921	14,712	
1985	32%	$760,621	97,575	22,060	
1986	19%	$907,519	118,494	28,632	
1987	5%	$954,995	126,519	32,163	
1988	17%	$1,119,684	150,367	39,971	
1989	32%	$1,480,623	201,125	55,402	2,000
1990	-3%	$1,438,144	197,031	55,680	1,940
1991	31%	$1,886,589	260,731	75,560	5,161
1992	8%	$2,039,676	283,749	83,765	7,734
1993	10%	$2,245,843	314,324	94,342	10,708
1994	2%	$2,292,800	322,651	98,268	12,962
1995	38%	$3,166,824	448,018	138,370	20,647
1996	23%	$3,897,654	553,522	172,656	27,856
1997	33%	$5,186,540	738,844	232,292	39,709
1998	28%	$6,641,331	948,281	299,894	53,387
1999	21%	$8,038,430	1,149,839	365,291	67,019
2000	-9%	$7,316,791	1,048,174	334,235	62,807
2001	-12%	$6,447,855	925,203	296,223	57,095
2002	-22%	$5,024,437	722,291	232,316	46,035
2003	29%	$6,459,474	930,787	301,119	61,730
2004	11%	$7,164,483	1,034,274	336,099	70,664
2005	5%	$7,512,677	1,084,540	352,433	74,098
2006	15%	$8,694,884	1,259,259	412,409	90,450
2007	5%	$9,163,538	1,327,133	434,638	95,325
2008	-39%	$5,601,431	813,388	268,074	60,754
2009	27%	$7,116,358	952,155	342,993	79,699
2010	15%	$8,186,112	1,097,278	396,742	93,954
2011	2%	$8,347,378	1,118,894	404,558	95,805
2012	16%	$9,666,264	1,295,679	468,478	110,942
2013	32%	$12,759,468	1,710,296	618,390	146,443
Avg.	12%	12%	11%	13%	11%

Ibbotson Associates **Stocks average 11.4% per year, bonds 5%, CDs 3%.** Stocks have gone up as much as 54% and as low as –43% in 1 year, up to 28% or down to –12% in 5 years, up 20% or down 0% in 10 years, up 18% or up 3% in 20 years. Short term bonds have gone up 14% or up 0% in 1 year, up 11% or up 0% in 5 years, up 9% or up 0% in 10 years, up 10% or up 1% in 20 years. Check: returns: http://www.moneychimp.com/features/market_cagr.htm

5

Low-cost beats high-cost

Cost Matters: 0.19% v 1.68%

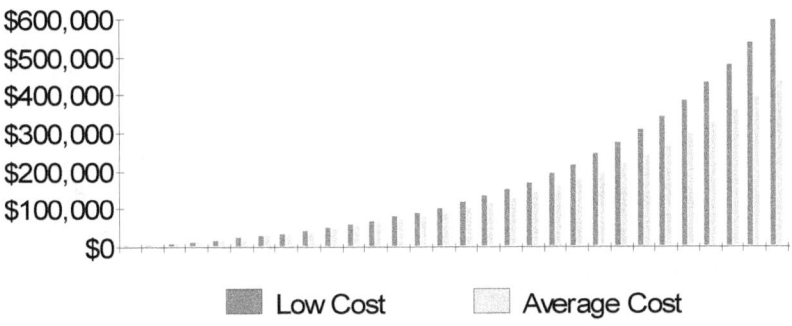

Low Cost   Average Cost

"In every single time period and data point tested,
***low-cost* funds beat high-cost funds."**

When I learned that the fund-rating analysts at <u>Morningstar</u> proved
that Wall Street is wrong about "professionally" managed funds
beating the market, I had a hard time believing that Wall Street had
been lying all my life. ***Low-cost*** funds always beat high-cost funds.
Predictors are paid to make educated guesses. No one can predict
the future. Your broker/advisor cannot beat a low-cost index.

The **best predictor** of your wealth-building success is COST. It
is common sense that there are just too many variables in the
success of growing companies' stocks for anyone to be able to pick
them in advance, consistently. A low-cost mutual fund provides the
best chance of maximizing our accumulations as the market leaders
change over time.

Contrary to Wall Street's BS, it does not matter which stocks
are rising or falling at any given time. If our account holds a broad
representation of stocks and our investment costs are low, we will

benefit over the long haul. We own them all!

Since the annual returns of all stocks average 10-12% over time, we want to pick the lowest cost mutual fund available. A stock fund that reflects an overall market is called an index fund. This kind of fund, explained below, costs only 0.05% ($5 per $10,000). Our account will compound at or near the 10-12% over time since ours costs 30-40 times less than Wall Street's. If we use the high-cost stock funds, we will earn only 6-8% over time. These funds pay managers high salaries with expensive bonuses. The fund owners and sales staff are paid well also. These funds are the cash cow of Wall Street.

The chart above makes it clear. Over time, the costs we pay each year may cut our total accumulation by over HALF. Instead of compounding at 10-12% annually on average, some people give up 1-3% of the earnings on their money to their middle person. They end up with less. They subsidize the Wall Street Wolf.

John Bogle, founder of the largest mutual fund firm, estimates that working people give up 63% of their total possible accumulations by paying 2% during their lifetimes. Costs include the manager, staff, trading, tax, holding cash for redemptions, etc.

Wall Street says that we can earn more by paying a 'star' manager to pick the right stocks on an ongoing basis. The money "experts" say we get what we pay for and a proven stock-picking manager will overcome the extra costs and make more for us.

The reality is that this **myth has been proven wrong**. The lowest cost funds don't pay a star manager and owner big bucks and so come out ahead over time. There are simply too many variables for anyone or computer program to pick the winning stocks *all the time*. Some of the lowest cost funds are called index funds. When we buy an market index, we are buying a piece of many companies. This gives us the same annual returns as the overall market over time. We pay tiny expenses so *We Keep More*!

Many studies have proven that index funds beat funds run by stock pickers most of the time. Low-cost index funds beat 86% of funds with a stock-picking manager.
http://www.financialsymmetry. com/deciding-whether-active-or-passive-funds-are-right-for-you/

When we investigate the experiences of the best money managers in the world, we find they recommend index funds to most people who invest as silent partners. Here are their statements:

Warren Buffett is probably history's greatest investor, in terms of results with $65 BILLION ($65 thousand million dollars) so far. He buys *companies* that provide valuable services to a great number of people. His company owns parts of Coke, GEICO, Fruit of the Loom, Benjamin Moore, Acme Bricks, Burlington Northern, etc. berkshirehathaway.com/

He told Reuters: "A very low-cost index is going to beat a majority of the amateur-managed money or professionally-managed money."

Compare the odds of selecting the correct mutual fund. A fund's chance of beating the market in EACH year is 3 out of 100. nytimes.com/2009/02/22/your-money/stocks-and-bonds/22stra.html

Peter Lynch, brilliant manager, Magellan Fund "…you'd be just as well off if you'd invested in the S&P 500." *One Up on Wall Street*, 1989, p. 240.

Jonathan Clements, formerly *The Wall Street Journal*
"Most people can do it themselves. ... By indexing, you don't just ensure that you will do better than most other investors. You will also enjoy the advantage of 'relative certainty.' . . . For most investors, Vanguard will be the place to go." *You've Lost It, Now What? How to beat the bear market and still retire on time*, 2003, p. 62, 70.

Charles D. Ellis, money managers' consultant
"The premise . . . that professional investment managers *can* beat the market . . . appears to be false. It is a loser's game. … clients would have done better in a market fund." Returns are "splendidly predictable—on average and over time." *Investment Policy, How to Win the Loser's Game*, 1985, p. 5, 20, 34.

Jane Bryant Quinn, consumer advisor
"I'm a longtime booster of index mutual funds. These funds follow the market as a whole. Tons of research has shown that most money managers don't beat the markets they invest in, after costs.

Maybe your own stocks or funds have excelled in the past couple of years. But in most cases, you've also been taking extra risk. The odds of superior performance are against you, in the long run. Indexing puts the odds on your side." *Los Angeles Business Journal*, May 8, 2000

Charles Schwab founder, discount broker
"I put my money where my mouth is: most of the mutual fund investments I have are in index funds, approximately 75%. My core investments are index funds. Experienced investors have discovered that in any given year, on average, only 20 to 30 percent of mutual funds outperform the market. That is why I recommend index funds…"
Mr. Schwab tells of one of his friends who owned many well-run funds. After keeping track of all the dividends, taxes, reinvestments tax basis and statements, he found he earned the same return as the index of these funds. After selling them all, he bought the index fund. He has "what he wanted in the first place: diversification, tax advantages, one statement, and lower expenses." *Guide to Financial Independence*, 1998, pp. 90, 103, 111.

Motley Fool, Internet site about investing
"Almost **everything** that you will ever read about mutual funds beyond, "Buy an index fund." is superfluous to your long-term success in investing in mutual funds." Fool.com.

Walter Updegrave, formerly senior editor, *Money*
"Mutual fund picking would be easier if there was one you could count on to outperform 70% or so of its competitors over long stretches of a decade or more. It's called an index fund. Although less than 10% of investors own an index fund, they are "one of the best-kept secrets" on Wall Street. My unabashed aim is to convince you to put at least a part of your money into one or more of these funds. You have a far less than a 50% chance of beating the market…. I strongly recommend that you make index funds your primary holding…." *The Right Way to Invest in Mutual Funds*, 1996, p 189-194.

Andrew Tobias, financial writer
"Scrimp and save, putting whatever you can into no-load, low-

expense stock market <u>index funds</u>, both U.S. and foreign. You will do better than 80% of your friends and neighbors." *My Vast Fortune*, 1997, p. 158.

There are many books written on the subject of index and "managed" funds. If you wish to vanquish the hype and understand investing, skim ***A Random Walk Down Wall Street*** by Princeton University's Burton Malkiel.

John Oliver gives you the short version:
<u>https://www.youtube.com/watch?v=GB4LgkGXN8Y</u> .

First, some fund managers do beat the market some of the time. There is no <u>proof</u> this can be done over time. <u>Yesterday's winners are usually tomorrow's losers.</u> The AVERAGE market return has been 10-12%, so a few managers will beat the average by luck— Just not the same ones every year. And we don't know in advance. nytimes.com/2008/07/13/business/13stra.html

Second, the costs of the manager, their staff and operations <u>must be paid for by you</u> whether or not they earn you a dime. <u>Costs can take 63% of our returns over time.</u> Surprisingly, while the stock index rose 11.11%, investors with high paid managers averaged only **3.69%** annually for 30 years ended 2013.
<u>DALBAR</u>'s annual QAIB

Third, high cost managers get paid for increasing the <u>size </u>of their funds, not for making you rich. Bringing in more money is a full-time job. It is inevitable that popular funds will grow until they produce average returns with high expenses. <u>Managers want to be rich</u>, not right. Salary: 1% of $1million or 1% or $200 million?

**"In every single time period and data point tested,
low-cost funds beat high-cost funds."**
http://www.cbsnews.com/news/morningstar-low-mutual-fund-fees-trump-our-star-ratings/

Basic fact
The best predictor of the success of a mutual fund is its cost.

6

Buy groups of stocks of growing companies

Range of annual returns of stocks, 1950 – 2000

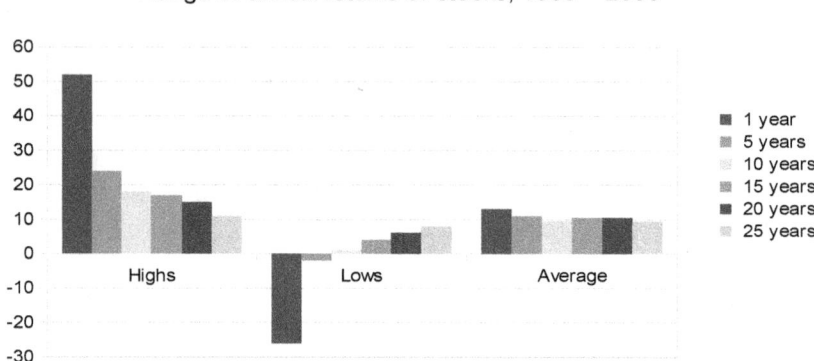

As I mentioned, Uncle Wei picked 12 stocks from the Dow because he said there are too many things that can go wrong with just one. There are always exceptions: Amazon's value went from $5,000 to $1 million. But few knew in advance. Would you have held on when it went from $85 to $6? There are fewer problems when you pick 12 of the best dividends payers of the Dow.

Later, in my career, I learned that the chance of picking one winning stock out of all of them is 1 in 3,000 *each* year. I also found that despite Wall Street hype, only 2.5% of the Street's "professionals," who hand-pick a bunch of stocks (a mutual fund), are successful over time. At their best, professionals who run the largest pension fund (CalPERS) could only earn 0% in fiscal 2015-16 while the market lost 1%.

So by picking 12 of the top long-term winners in the Dow, I had a better chance of success over time. My probability was higher (98%) than picking just one new highly-touted stock like MGIC Investment. It would be easier to know in advance that one company could make me rich in 20 years but research shows that none of the gurus in finance has ever done that—even Mr Buffett.

Uncle Wei convinced me by age 18 that owning 12 solid companies with profits paid as quarterly dividends was the only **"guarantee" of success** anyone can manage. He used the analogy of a molecule of water in a stream. Most would make it to the sea. Some would be eaten by a big fish.

Picking *individual* stocks as a strategy is NOT likely to work for us. The odds of me beating all the professional managers are tiny, unless I have insider information like Congress people do. Our strategy is to build wealth as a **silent partner** in growing global companies. As the founder of the largest mutual fund firm, John Bogle, says: "Don't look for the needle. Buy the haystack."

When I worked on Wall Street, I saw how the 'professionals' *manipulated partial truths* about their products in order to sell them. They make their living claiming to find the "needle" every year. It is the same deceit as state lottery games. We kid ourselves into thinking that "someone has to win, why not me." Our chance of winning is so low it is a waste of money.

Gambling is what most of Wall Street is about—separating people from their money with the illusion of riches. I learned from receiving dividends every quarter that all I had to do was keep reinvesting them and add my birthday money and I would actually have real "winnings." And the more money I put in when I got my first job, the more my account was worth.

At parties, I would hear how much savings my friends had and it was a whole lot less than my account. I didn't want to change my relationship with my girlfriend, so I didn't tell her (until later). When we got married and bought a house in 1985, we could easily afford the down payment. I had about $150,000 in my account.

We continued to invest in my Uncle's choice companies. We switched the account to a low-cost broker, Charles Schwab in 1985 or '86. We also funded our employer's 401k accounts. They were a supplement to pensions in the 80s. We both had well-paying jobs so we made investing a priority over other things. We used lower-cost mutual funds because we calculated that we would give up at least HALF our total nest egg if we paid an advisor 2% annually.

You can see our progress in reaching our goals in the account history displayed previously. We used our brokerage account balance to buy used cars, fix our home and take vacations. The account balances let us carry high deductibles for car, home and health insurance. We bought $500,000 in term insurance in case one of us was not around. It cost under $30 a month in our 30s and 40s. It was cheap because there is little chance of dying that young. We dropped this coverage when we hit age 55. We had enough in our investment accounts if something should happen to us. Our kids were on their own by then.

In the 80s, I used my HP 17b to estimate how much our accounts would be worth in the future if we moved our money to Schwab and stopped paying our broker. Today I use an online compounding calculator. You can see that your accumulation drops to $0.7 million if you pay a 2% fee to any middleman. You earn 8% instead of 10% annually. You could have $1 million in about 33 years at 10% using low-cost funds, no tax and no trading.
http://www.moneychimp.com/calculator/compound_interest_calculator.htm

Middlemen always say that you don't want to invest in market index funds because they produce **only** average (mediocre) returns. The part they don't mention is that 10-12% a year over time is more likely than their illusion of Wall Street riches. Investing in companies inside an index provides no guaranteed return but the average returns have held steady since the 1930s when they started keeping records. No "professional" can make that claim.

The brilliant stock pickers have come and gone. My clients have used these Vanguard mutual funds and have earned over 11% for a long time. Most started with the 500 Index and added companies in the Energy, Health and International sectors.

2015 Total Return	Fund	Long-term Return	Longevity
1.4%	500 Index	10.8%*	since 1976
-21.5%	Energy	10.3%	since 1984
-3.3%	Extended Market Idx	10.6%	since 1987
12.7%	Health	17.3%	since 1984
-0.7%	International Growth	10.3%	since 1981
2.6%	PRIMECAP	13.5%	since 1984
-3.6%	Small Cap Index	10.5%	since 1960
1.3%	Wellesley Income	9.9%	since 1970
-3.3%	Windsor	11.3%	since 1958
-3.2%	Windsor II	10.6%	since 1985
-1.7%	Average	11.5%	

*Average Annual Returns as of 12/31/15.

You can see that some companies and even sectors lose money some years but over time the average holds. These Top Ten funds provide you with the alternative to the fact that no manager can pick winners all the time. Generally, each part of the market has good times and bad. Because you own them all, you have some assurance of on-going positive returns.

2013 Total Return	Fund	Long-term Return*	Longevity
32.3%	500 Index	11.0%*	since 1976
18.4%	Energy	13.2%	since 1984
38.4%	Extended Market Idx	11.2%	since 1987
43.2%	Health	17.1%	since 1984
23.0%	International Growth	11.2%	since 1981
39.7%	PRIMECAP	13.7%	since 1984
37.6%	Small Cap Index	10.9%	since 1960
9.2%	Wellesley Income	10.1%	since 1970
36.1%	Windsor	11.6%	since 1958
30.7%	Windsor II	11.1%	since 1985
30.9%	Average	12.1%	

*Average Annual Returns as of 12/31/13.

Continuity means you can't trade on tips from brokers or try to time the market sectors. That doesn't work. But if you are a long-term investor, not speculator, it doesn't matter what happens in any year.

Basic fact: growing companies create wealth. Low-cost mutual funds inside a tax-FREE account that is automatically funded every month is your best chance of reaching your goals.

You need broad diversification. Verify this by looking at the history of the returns of each asset classes (https://www.hennion andwalsh.com/wpcontent/uploads/2016/01/2015CallanTable.pdf). You have a choice. You can go with the averages that have been consistently earning over 10% or try your salesman's strategy with 3.79% ON AVERAGE over time. Sales people cannot 'guarantee' any specific return *by law* for good reason.

The easiest way to begin is to save $500 a month in our savings account until we have the $1,000 minimum for Vanguard's entry funds: STAR #56 or Target Date 2060 #1691. We can open the Roth IRA by phone or online: STAR minimum is $1,000. Most Vanguard funds need $3,000 to start. We can keep contributing to this index fund until we have $3,000 for the 500 Index and then $3,000 for the Extended Market funds. Vanguard's licensed staff: 800.551.8631. STAR has returned nearly10% since 1985.

The second way to begin is to open a Roth IRA at TIAA, the world's largest pension company, primarily for educational and research institutions. Low expenses and low initial contributions make TIAA an organization we can stay with for life. TIAA 's licensed representatives: 800.842.2888.

At TIAA.org, we can make application and begin immediately with an automatic monthly contribution of $100 or more from our bank account. We can follow how the assets grow by themselves. TIAA has funds that provide us with the diversity of companies worldwide: TIAA Equity Index is the first.

Request a *prospectus* (owner's manual) for each fund you will be using at Vanguard or TIAA. Both mutual fund firms have experienced salaried representatives that provide accurate information about accounts and funds. Both offer low-cost index funds that hold a broad representation of the market returns of 10-12%. This is a building block to accumulating wealth.

Both firms are focused on you, not on profits.

Basic facts

Using these funds provides you with returns of 10-12% annually on average with the benefit of avoiding single company or industry failures. They provide exposure to new growth potential around the world with less risk than holding one company, one sector, or one country. They provide low-cost index and managed fund with proven track records.

7

Spend less than you earn

The Value of Starting Early

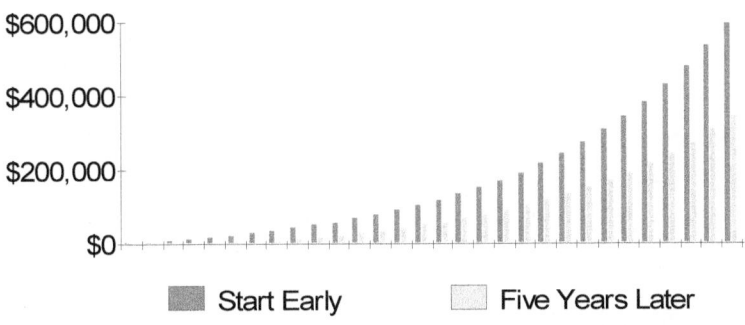

I was lucky because I started the investing habit early. The birthday gift was a surprise and I had no bills to pay at age 12, ha ha. I could invest because my Uncle Wei did it with me. I was mesmerized by the promise that I could ***own*** part of GE, Sears, Coke, Kodak, etc.

I learned to invest early so I always made it a priority. I was lucky in that I had a job most of my life and could afford to invest. In order to reach any money goal, we need to find at least $250 per month to invest. We can build wealth by following the strategy outlined in the previous chapters, but we need to have at least $250 available in the first place.

In my first job, I wanted to buy a car and pay my loans. I had to choose. The loans seemed to be important. Getting rid of them seemed less important than getting a car though. Also I reasoned that I could wait to invest.

Well, Uncle Wei found out and showed me what waiting can do to my plan to have a $1,000,000. By waiting to invest we give up almost HALF of our final total after 30 years. He then helped me find a car pool to ride to work and offered to loan me his BMW whenever I needed it for a special occasion.

Yes I was lucky for someone to help me keep investing. He said most people plan to invest but never seem to make it a priority to start or keep going. He told me that he keeps a list of his goals on his fridge to remind him when he starts thinking of buying something. He puts it on the list, usually making it less of a priority than reaching his other goals—home, business, car, vacation.

Compounding does not perform its miracle if we interrupt the flow of cash. In this way he said, my goals can include all that I want, in time. Later, after I had built up a sizable balance, I could start buying the things on my list. My old list is below:

Priorities	Time
$1,000,000	By 2000
Home	1985
Used car	1980
New furniture	1987
Vacation to China	1997
Start business	2000

My wife and I eventually got what we wanted and more. Investing is like running a business. You have to keep at it. Wei said the only thing we have to supply is patience. We followed his simple steps as I explained above.

First, we made investing automatic—out of sight—it runs itself. We do nothing in our investment accounts. If we ran short of money in one month, we skipped something else—we brought our lunch for a month for instance. We cut subcriptions we did not use. We gave up our box at the bank. We cut our trips when gas prices were high. I quit smoking at age 37.

Second, we went through our insurance needs with Uncle Wei. We raised deductibles on car, home and health policies. This cut premiums. We dropped some coverage like our kid's policies and cancer coverage. We cut expenses for car washes, monthly dining, shopping, etc.

Our family agreed on these measures and our own individual initiatives—clipping coupons, working overtime on occasion— would be worth it to reach the goals we laid out. We didn't feel bad if we couldn't buy something right away. We both agreed to put it on the list. This kept us from getting angry we didn't have something we really wanted, like a big screen.

This spending-investing plan works for all types of goals. I have asked my clients to make written plans like ours so that they don't fight over saving-spending decisions. For every use of their investment account, they had to consider the tax consequences.

Today, we use and I recommend the Roth IRA. You can borrow your contributions without taxes anytime. However, you must increase the amount you invest to make up for this money as long as the amount is less than $5,500 ($6,500 over age 50) a year.

Clients have used their long-term accumulation account for vacations, cars, appliances, emergencies, etc. This works if they pay their accounts back. After age 59.5, there are no taxes at all— NEVER. However, to meet our long-term goals, we have to pay ourselves back quickly to take advantage of compounding.

I now give clients *The Insiders' Guides to Buying Discount Financial Services: Buy Direct and Save $3,000 Every Year*. It provides an easy way to save $3,000 or more on financial products they already use. There are buyer's *Guides* for each specific area. We review some of the ways to find $250 in savings in the next chapter.

Basic fact

You can't spend more than you earn and at the same time become an owner of growing companies. Even if you did not start early, you can build a fortune over time with compounding of your contributions.

Are you paying too much?

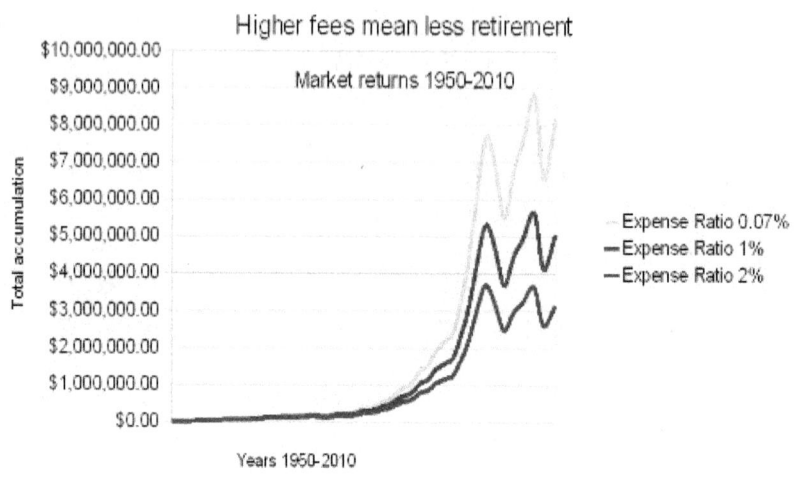

Higher fees mean less retirement

Market returns 1950-2010

Total accumulation

$10,000,000.00
$9,000,000.00
$8,000,000.00
$7,000,000.00
$6,000,000.00
$5,000,000.00
$4,000,000.00
$3,000,000.00
$2,000,000.00
$1,000,000.00
$0.00

Years 1950-2010

Expense Ratio 0.07%
Expense Ratio 1%
Expense Ratio 2%

8

Buy only the services you need

I was lucky. My uncle taught me how to build wealth from an early age. I did not have to give up anything to start growing my fortune. I started early. By age 30, I already had half a million. It takes 7-9 years to accumulate $1 million if we already have $500,000.

Uncle Wei convinced me by age 15 that being an owner of company stock was the way to get rich. I was interested in how the 12 companies made money because I got paid for loaning them money—dividends. My account grew. This was my incentive to invest—buying only what I needed as I grew up. I went to a state college. I did NOT live in a fraternity. I did NOT blow my student loans on beer, parties, or books I could borrow.

Today I help clients see that they must "REDIRECT" the **cash they already spend** on things they really don't need or can buy for less. This is where their future comes from. Most of us waste $3,000 or more each year on financial services and *stuff*.

For instance, the difference between paying full price for a new car and a 3-year-old model with more gadgets can be 40% or more. When we put our future on top of our priority list, we can REDIRECT the savings to a more worthwhile purpose.

It is the same with financial services. Most of us are not used to shopping for cars, insurance, mutual funds, banking and mortgages. So we don't. But look at the <u>annual savings</u>:

Auto insurance: save $400 or more EVERY year by changing/dropping some extras we don't need.

Home insurance: save $200 or more EVERY year by changing one limit.

Life insurance: save $1,000 or more EVERY year by using direct to consumer insurer and low-cost 10-year term.

Mutual funds: save $2-3,000 EVERY year by using a low-cost

provider not a sales person.

Banking: save $120 EVERY year by using a low-cost provider of the benefits we usually use.

Mortgage: save $2,000 on closings and lower interest rates.

Investments: earn 15-30% guaranteed just by paying off credit cards too.

Tax refund: average $3,052 can pay for $1 million retirement.

Using the ***The Insiders' Guides to Buying Discount Financial Services: Buy Direct and Save $3,000 Every Year*** I helped compile, you can REDIRECT the $250 a month without having to give up anything important. We don't need to 'tighten our belts' or make a budget. We can give up things we would not benefit from anyway.

Dan Keppel, my colleague, gives these examples from people who have told about their experience using the ***Guides***.

George B. New York:
"I saved $1,356 on my vehicle insurance using your Insider's Guide to Vehicle Insurance. I saved by using some of your Insiders' 'tricks of the trade' like dropping the extras that I already had."

John D. New York:
"I canceled my life insurance and used the money to buy the mutual funds. You were right. I didn't need the insurance anymore. My kids are all grown. My new wife and I invest as much as we can now. Your Guide to 'Living' Insurance is a great way to look at our insurance needs."

Mark K. Ohio:
"I had no idea how to invest in the 401k that my new job offered. I have not been disappointed with the mutual funds suggested by other members. I saved about a $1,000 by transferring my old 401k mutual funds to the low-cost funds in your Guide. When I sold my primary residence in 2004, I followed members' advice with the gains. I use all your Guides to help me save more for my retirement since I got a late start. Thanks."

Example:

MetLife charged $983 for a $300,000 30-year **term policy**. This same $300,000 benefit was sold by Savings Bank Life Insurance for $384 a year. Their financial strength ratings are A+ and their underwriting requirements are the same. The difference, $599, over 30 years is $17,970. If invested, this difference can add $175,000 to OUR **account**.

Unfortunately, people pick name brands instead of shopping for services they need. Companies know this and spend a lot for TV advertising and gimmicks that cost you.

Basic fact

We already spend the money we could use to become wealthy. We buy financial services we don't need. I know because I work with clients and see the waste. When we learn to shop—getting value for our money—we redirect money already in our budget to creating our future happiness. We can give up high-cost brokers, advisors, agents and other sales people.

If you could earn $175,000 by shopping for an hour, wouldn't you do it?

Look at what can happen to your account!

Monthly Accumulation at 12% per year									
	5	10	15	20	25	30	35	40	45	50
$100	$8,167	$23,004	$49,958	$98,925	$187,884	$349,496	$643,095	$1,176,477	$2,145,469	$3,905,834
$200	$16,334	$46,008	$99,916	$197,850	$375,768	$698,992	$1,286,190	$2,352,954	$4,290,938	$7,811,668
$300	$24,501	$69,012	$149,874	$296,775	$563,652	$1,048,488	$1,929,285	$3,529,431	$6,436,408	$11,717,502
$500	$40,835	$115,020	$249,790	$494,625	$939,420	$1,747,480	$3,215,475	$5,882,385	$10,727,346	$19,529,169

The Roth IRA Rules

Contributions:

$5,500 ($6,500 over age 50) each year
Income under $132,000 (2016) single
married $194,000 (2016)

Distributions:

Tax-FREE for contributions.
And Tax-FREE for earnings if
Over age 591/2,
Account open 5 years,
Taxable earnings unless
Disabled,
First home ($10,000),
Death

Bonus:

Account can grow tax-FREE for life
Distribution at age 70.5 not required
Heirs don't pay income tax
Account has no maximum

Check with your tax preparer
https://www.irs.gov/publications/p590a/

9

Manage the account only once a year

We continue to make more money when **_snoring_** than when active.

Warren Buffett

After Uncle Wei, this is the advice I follow. This is the advice of the most successful investor of our day. He is making it clear that we should NOT touch our investments very often. Contrary to the advice of the Wall Street 'professionals,' Buffett leaves his assets alone to compound over time. He does not follow the 'hot' investment of the day. He buys the stock of growing companies around the world. He has held some investments for over 40 years —Coke, GEICO, AmEx, WellsFargo.

Our emotions tell us to sell when our account balance goes down. We want to buy the next investment hit to make up for our previous losses. This is why we have a hard time following Buffett's advice. However, the emotions that cause us to be bad investors are what we can control—not the stock price of growing companies worldwide.

Patience is a habit we can learn.

Our contributions to our account need to be automatic so we **buy more shares when the market is down** and less when it is up. I control my emotions by reviewing the line graph of investment choices below. If we sell we may miss the next advance. This is when I remember Warren Buffett's advice: "**our favorite holding period is forever**." http://www.berkshirehathaway.com/letters/1988.html

When we own the whole stock market, we really **don't have to worry** about buying and selling our mutual funds. There is no better investment for the long term. Stocks are the safest investment for periods over 10 years. Patience is profitable.

Look at client Tom's account. He got to $3 million and then "lost" a million but he did not panic and sell. He got back to $3 million. I don't sell my stocks because there is no safer investment. If I need money to buy a new used car or fix my home or take a vacation, I have the money. I don't have to worry because I already saved for a "rainy" day. I don't need an emergency fund because I have my retirement accounts—brokerage, IRA and Roth IRA.

Today, I am still making contributions because I am still working in my own business. Once a year, I compare the total account balance to where I think it should be. I note what happened during the year for any one fund. I go to the Vanguard site and read about that fund. Do I need to make a change? No, usually I don't. I use the 10 funds listed above. They have consistently done well over the years. I put new money in <u>Energy</u>—the one on sale.

I don't believe in re-balancing so there is no need to sell funds that have done well in order to re-balance the 10 funds' balances equally. Most of the research shows that re-balancing each year does not change the long-term outcome of the whole portfolio. Some clients use their contributions each year to add to the fund that has grown the **least**. However, as each fund becomes larger, the effect of adding contributions becomes smaller over time. In retirement, I shift more from stock to the <u>Wellesley Income</u> fund.

When we have to sell shares to meet an emergency or avoid interest payments by using cash for large ticket items, we may sell shares in the fund with the largest dollar value. This is a better strategy than selling shares in all funds since we don't know which fund may recover the fastest going forward.

Basic fact

Our tax-FREE retirement income account does not require us to hire an advisor to manage it. Advisors do not know what the future holds anymore than we do so paying them 1-3% each year just reduces our annual returns. Their fees/charges can take up to 63% of our total accumulations over time. We are silent partners in growing businesses around the world.

This is how we create ***Wealth.***

It is easy if we learn patience.

It is hard because we must control our emotions.

Where do you want your balance to be?

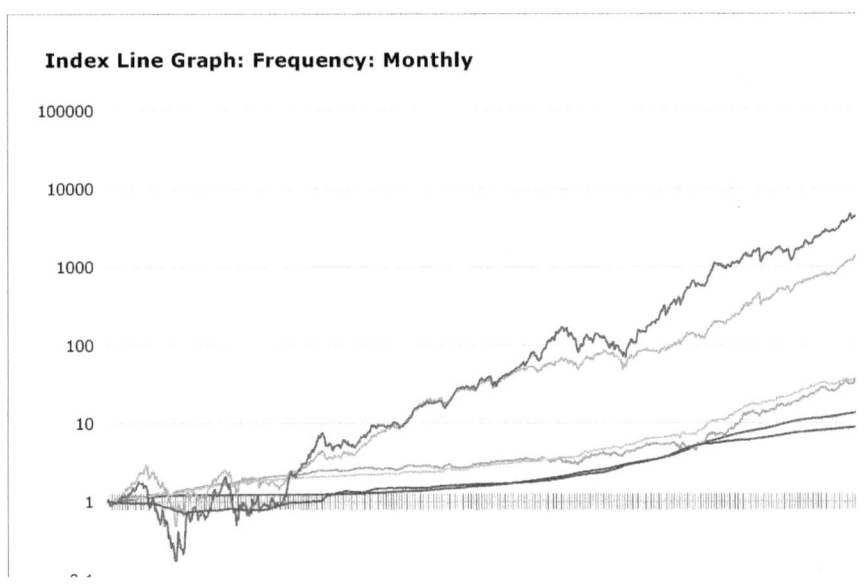

Top line—Small Cap Stocks
2nd line—Large Cap Stocks (S&P 500)
3rd line—US Long-term Corporate Bonds
4th line—Intermediate-term Government Bonds
5th line—US 30 day Government T-bills
6th line—US inflation

Courtesy: Dr. Campbell R. Harvey http://www.duke.edu/~charvey/

Your 'Action' Plan
This is how to build wealth:

This week:
Goal
Set up Roth IRA and start automatic contributions with trustee

This month:
Goal
Do Nothing with investments; don't watch

Next month:
Goal
Do Nothing with investments; don't listen to market media

This year:
Goals
Check fund totals and redirect automatic contributions if necessary

2nd year:
Goals
Check fund totals and redirect automatic contributions if necessary

3rd year:
Goals
Check fund totals and redirect automatic contributions if necessary

4th year:
Goals
Check fund totals and redirect automatic contributions if necessary

Every year:
Goals
Check fund totals and redirect automatic contributions if necessary

10

Live well in your life

I was lucky. I learned the **5 basic facts** about money so I did not have to worry about having money during my life and in "retirement." I am retired from the 9-5 obligations. I am now 8-6 doing what I enjoy—helping others learn the 5 basic facts about money. I also do taxes in the AARP tax-aide program.

Our schools could and should be doing this so that more people can enjoy life and not worry about money. I ask every person I help to listen to Earl Crawley: https://www.youtube.com/watch?v=XD0svDGyLWU. He may be a parking attendant who never earned more than $12 an hour but Mr. Earl has accumulated a portfolio of stocks and bonds worth over $600,000. It took time.

I want each person to know that their goals are not impossible. If Mr. Earl can do it, they can do it.

Anybody can by using the **5 basic facts** to make your life goals reality. Every person applies the use of money differently. Today when I read that "Wall Street fell" on the news Britain might leave the EU, I got on my computer and moved money into stocks. *"Attention Wal-Mart shoppers"* there is a sale on stocks in isle 4, 5, 6, and 7. How many people do that? The only people the media is talking about are money managers who think they can avoid a downturn—sell high then buy low. However, you and I know that they may miss the high the next day. And they did miss it because stocks went up the next day. Plus you have to pay commissions on the trades and the taxes when they sell.

I can afford to do this buying because I don't have to worry about money now. Uncle Wei taught me by age 25 that when I have extra money, I should buy more stock of the 12 companies because we know they are strong and will prosper for another 100 years. When the price of Coke or GE or the others goes down, we have a rare opportunity to live better in the future. Those extra shares I got for $2,000 in 1978 went up over 5,800%.

And I only have to pay tax on those gains if I sell the shares. Basically, I have a tax-FREE account in my brokerage account. I have paid tax on the dividends as I got them, so I can chose when I want to pay tax on the appreciation of the value of the shares. If bought them at $6 I will owe gains tax on the rise to $50.

Why would I sell? There are few better companies. When I need money to travel to a financial conference I can sell 50 shares and pay less tax percentage-wise than when I worked. The gains rate is 15% compared to 34% total tax on my salary when I worked for other owners.

I don't sell because I have a business and can deduct the cost of the travel and conference and vehicles and many other things. I don't need to touch the investments in my broker account. I pay no tax on withdrawals from my ROTH IRA. I have to pay tax on the mandatory withdrawals from my IRA after age 70.

I strongly suggest using the ROTH for anyone I work with because there is no federal or state tax after age 59.5. The IRS §408 trust account allows withdrawals of contributions anytime. And I can leave the balance to all my grandchildren without a trust. http://www.irs.gov/retirement/article/0,,id=137307,00.html

Some clients have moved some of their accumulations into tax-FREE bond funds in order to provide a monthly income to their checking account. They created a retirement spending plan that assured them of that monthly income of a fixed dollar amount with this Guide: amazon.com/Your-Retirement-Spending-Plan-enough

We don't know what will happen to Social Security by 2038. We don't know what employer pensions might look like by then. I am assuming that inflation will continue at a 3% rate so I show people they must stay invested in stocks for at least 50% of their funds. If they are in retirement for 20 years, the buying power of their nest egg is cut in half by then.

Uncle Wei warned me not to count on employer pensions. He saw them destroyed by the adoption of 401ks which require us—

not employers—to pay. Now young people may not even be in a 401k long enough to build a nest egg. Some jobs don't come with a matching benefit. A Roth IRA is better than a matchless 401k.

When I was working, I used a self-funded IRA and then ROTH IRA since my later jobs did not have matching and I did not like the fees of the 401k options. Most of my investments are in IRA or rollover IRA (from former 401k) accounts. Most of the IRA money is taxable as income (to 33%) not capital gains (15%). I took no deduction for some of it but the rollover money is all taxable.

I have to watch how I access it because when you take this money it is added to other income and to SS benefits for tax rate calculations. I will take some of it each year and pay tax at a lower rate than taking it all in one year. I need to calculate how much SS is taxed based on this amount too since up to 85% of benefits are taxable. These are just math problems that we can easily fix.

Over most of my life I have lived well because I had my accounts to fall back on if I needed them. Most people don't have these simply because our schools do not teach *investing* at all. If I had not started early I would be at about HALF my goal level.

Another way I convince young people to start early is with this chart: http://www.saferchild.org/power/. If invested by age 26, most adults would have no problem living their life without the fear of NOT having money.

It is true that inflation cuts the value of your account over time but having $500,000 would be better than the average nest egg of $172,000 most of us have. If we take out 4% a year, we will have about $7,000 per year for living expenses. Even if we add SS benefits of $16,000, that's not enough for most people.

Our society has not chosen to teach investing in school so the end result will be a difficult life for most. The alternative could be a nest egg that produces $30,000 real income for life. Some clients transfer some of their money into a balanced fund like *Wellesley Income* in order to generate the income for the coming year. The balance of their tax-FREE account remains in the broad market funds we have listed above.

These funds may continue to produce returns in the 10-12% range. If there is a bad year like 2008, we are not taking money out of our principal at a bad time. We take the money from the Wellesley Income fund with 60% income-earning bonds with 9-10% total return since 1970.

The funds we have listed above include some of the most consistent low volatility returns over time. The ***Wellesley Income*** fund has <u>produced about 10% per year</u> on average since 1970. It contains stocks and bonds. **This fund alone might be our source** of annual withdrawals of interest and dividends. Since our **account** is not taxable, there are no tax considerations in the decision of which fund to tap for our monthly income.

If the people I work with use the ROTH for most of their working lives, they will have no tax liability on this income of up to $4,000 per month. They can avoid tax on Social Security and/or our qualified retirement funds too.

The tax-FREE income will provide most of our needs. If we continue to follow the same strategy, we will find a comfortable lifestyle throughout the 30 to 40 years of not working unless we want to.

I and many clients are assuming we will work at least part time after we take full retirement and begin collecting Social Security. If <u>benefits are cut by Congress,</u> we will need to work. We are encouraged to use our tax-FREE income to develop a small business since this can help us control the income that is taxed.

We may find that we will have a sizable legacy as we age. There are many ways to pass on our wealth that don't require attorney fees and complicated legal formulations. Many clients have found that incremental gifts to charity and family provide immediate gratification. They have used the suggestions for wealth transfer presented in the ***Retirement Spending Plan***.
amazon.com/Your-Retirement-Spending-Plan-enough/dp/1461084016/

Basic fact

Our retirement income can be tax-FREE and can have the purchasing power of about $40,000 in today's dollars. Wealthy people who actually earned it don't go out and buy a mansion and the trappings of the wealthy when they retire. They usually have paid off their homes. They travel and share with family. Some continue to earn income doing what they enjoy or provide help to others in their volunteer efforts. Our nest egg and all the earnings are TAX-FREE. We can spend it all!

How to Buy Securities For Retirement

1. Cost matters: Broker/advisor cost 1% to 3% for each of you

   If you use a salesperson, fees can cost HALF A NEST EGG!
   $6,000 per year @11% for 28 years = $1,064,740
   $6,000 per year @11-1% for 28 years = $885,795
   $6,000 per year @11-2% for 28 years = $738,807
   $6,000 per year @11-3% for 28 years = $617,570

2. Broker/advisor stock picking does not beat index funds over the long run. No money manager has been able to beat the market consistently. **No one can forecast the future**.

3. Compounding is the key to investment success. The chance of you buying AND selling, both, at the right times, is near zero. Time and patience pay.

4. A Tax-FREE investment account increases your balance 25%.

5. Putting all your money in one stock or market sector guarantees failure over time. No one investment is perfect.

6. 'Dollar cost average' buying technique lowers the cost of shares over time. When you invest a fixed amount each month, you buy more mutual fund shares when the price is low and less when high. Over time, you will own more shares at a lower average cost.

7. If you don't have 28 years, convert part of your 401k or IRA to a Roth IRA each year, paying tax annually. Retirement can last 30!

8. Market down? Look at Tom's account balances again.

Let money work for you

What was hard about that? The mechanics of investing are simple. The *hard part is controlling our emotions*. Why can't we share the basic facts about money in high school? Are the schools afraid to offend the financial industry? Do the people who write the math curriculum know nothing about money? I remember my high school algebra, trig and geometry but I don't remember money compounding being taught. I was lucky I had Uncle Wei.

Investing is not taught because schools would be sued after the first drop in stock prices. We don't teach patience. Investing is really about owning a company for the long haul and you could lose money. But, there is no better **LONG-term** investment than stocks. Buying a **low-cost** stock mutual fund of many firms goes a long way to solving that problem.

But it doesn't solve it like teaching bank savings does. So schools teach savings and short-term thinking. We don't learn patience. And **compounding** requires patience. So does building a business. You don't learn about building a business until you have to learn from necessity. You can get an MBA but even then they emphasize quarterly earnings not success over time.

I was lucky that someone gave me lessons over time so that they could explain why a certain stock price goes down. Uncle Wei explained that **price is not value**. Price won't change a firm's prospects. Actually, this is the Buffett story. He is the good steward —a fiduciary—of his stockholder's money. He buys more when others panic and sell. How does he keep his head? He knows the business well enough to see past the short-term and go long for the real value of the firm.

I learned that we must let money work for us. How does money work for us? It compounds itself. At each birthday, I invested $25 in a company that paid a dividend and that each year those dividends buy more shares and each year the dividends got larger.

I learned that I reduced the risk of losing money by owning 12

different successful companies. I invested once a year keeping costs low. Later I would buy mutual fund shares run by the low-cost leading fund company. Later, I would save even more by using a **tax-FREE account** so I avoided taxes on gains each year AND later when I took money out of the account.

When I got a full time job I used the **automatic investing** feature of my 401k plan. Automatically, my plan deducted $125 from my paycheck for my investment option of a broad stock index fund. I never missed my goal of investing a set amount each month. When prices were low, I bought more shares with my $250 a month. When they were high, I bought fewer shares.

I never stopped investing even when my broker suggested I switch to high paying CDs (in the 1980s), annuities (in the 90s) or use leverage from a margin account. After I left my brokerage firm and transferred my accounts to Vanguard, I still had the trustee debit my checking account monthly to invest in mutual funds.

I had my employers send my pension and 401k accounts to Vanguard so that all my investing was in the low-cost leader. I have one statement with my 7 figure balances and tax information easy to check once a year.

I got to 7 figures by letting my money work—compound--without "managing" it. Despite Wall Street's claims, none of their smart people can know everything and predict the next Apple or Amazon. I learned to ignore the hype of Wall Street media because I worked there. I saw the fees, commissions and charges that made the firm and their owners wealthy. The industry takes an estimated $560 billions year after year from many people who can ill afford it. Because of the way they work, the average brokerage customer earns just 3.79%. Trading stocks does NOT benefit them. Most people act like gamblers in a casino not like business owners. pbs.org/moyers/journal/09282007/

Uncle Wei prepared me for my future by spending time to show me how to be a successful investor. We must be patient for our 'businesses' to grow and make us successful. You can't inherit money smarts. Most people who inherit money blow it before long. http://www.wsj.com/articles/SB10001424127887324662404578334663271139552.

Wei showed me to recognize that we can't know everything about investing. There is no way we can know the future: It is impossible to predict a successful company or fund manager. The wise learn not to try. That's *The Losers Game*.

https://www.ifa.com/pdfs/ellis_charles_the_losers_game_1975.pdf

It is hard to be patient and let our money grow by itself. Most people don't have the experience with a business or stocks of companies they know. They don't see the market the way that Warren Buffett does. They see it as a casino where the lucky win or a black hole where they can lose their life savings.

A person paying 1-3% of their nest egg every year to an advisor can't then admit they get very little for their money. Most advisors can't beat the investment return of the market so that $3-5,000 a year in fees is just paying the Wall Street Wolf. Over time that fee goes up and can take up to 63% of our total possible accumulations. Advisors like to buy and sell securities creating taxes and commissions that don't help us. Large pensions don't trade stocks. businessweek.com/articles/2013-01-24/

The key to reaching our goal of $1,000,000 is compounding of high returns over time. We can get there by becoming patient business owners. Brokers and advisors are sales people. Sales people take fees, charged, etc. Sales people don't give refunds if they don't beat the market! Avoid their mistakes.

The clear **winning strategy** is to do nothing. Set up your investment plan to automatically buy low-cost stock funds and let compounding work its miracle. Over time using a tax-FREE account with low costs, we can accumulate enough from $250 a month each at 10-12%. Using a compounding calculator, we find http://www.moneychimp.com/calculator/compound_interest_calculator.htm, the range is about 33 years. If each spouse has an account, we can be assured of enough income no matter how long each of us lives.

Most people are NOT going to be successful at this because they are impatient and don't let compounding do the work. They listen to Wall Street "professionals" who make a living promising to beat the market with no losses. They pay high fees and taxes for this advice that is wrong. By using the **5 basic facts**, we avoid the fees, taxes, and bad timing. No one can predict the future but a bunch of successful companies has produced 10-12% so far. We will never be taxed on this account—it is like Uncle Sam "giving" us $300,000! We avoid the 25% Fed and 5-7% tax of most states on income from our $1 million account.

We don't teach the **5 basic facts** in high school: compounding, low-cost, stock index funds, automatic, tax-FREE.

You must take the first step. Call Vanguard or TIAA yourself to set up your account. It takes about an hour to set up a Roth IRA for each of you. You can do it online or by phone with a licensed rep.

There is a clear reason why some become wealthy. It is neither luck nor inheritance. Millions of immigrants to this country have done it before. They lived below their means. They saved and invested in businesses they worked. They did not let temporary cash flow problems stop them from building wealth. They used this same strategy by any other name, every day.

As many clients say, "I never even miss the contributions because I never see them. Then all of a sudden, I see my statement" [has $25,000, $50,000, $250,000, $1,000,000.] "We are talking real money here." *Set it and forget it.*

Can you do NOTHING?

Call to set up your accounts and then let your money grow

Call Vanguard 800.551.8631 or TIAA-CREF 800.842.2888 today.
https://investor.vanguard.com/what-we-offer/iras/traditional-iras-and-roth-iras

or
https://www.TIAA-cref.org/public/pdf/mfirains.pdf

NOTES

Priorities   Timeline

Gifts to others   _____

Retirement $1 million   _____

Home   _____

College   _____

_____   _____

_____   _____

_____   _____

The Author

Zhou Wang has been in financial services for over 20 years. He was a managing executive of the sales units of a number of firms. He is one of the insiders who contributed to the *The Insiders Guides* set of buyers' guides edited by Dan Keppel. The guides provide specific ways to save on all financial services. ***The Insiders' Guides to Buying Discount Financial Services: Buy Direct and Save $3,000 Every Year*** is available at Amazon, Barnes & Noble, Junglee, bookadda, allbookstores, ebay, fishpond, alibris, powells, booksamillion, etc

To receive a weekly Alert with wealth-building ideas, go to www.TheInsidersGuides.com

www.ingramcontent.com/pod-product-compliance
Lightning Source LLC
Chambersburg PA
CBHW070227210526
45169CB00023B/991